MW01152068

All-In-One Piano Lessons

Book C

Authors
**Barbara Kreader, Fred Kern,
Phillip Keveren, Mona Rejino**

Consultants
Tony Caramia, Bruce Berr,
Richard Rejino

Manager, Educational Piano
Jennifer Linn

Editor
Anne Wester

Illustrator
Fred Bell

FOREWORD

Building on the success of the **All-In-One Piano Lessons Books A** and **B**, the **All-In-One Piano Lessons Books C** and **D** combine selected pages from the original Level 2 Piano Lessons, Technique, Solos, Theory Workbook, and Practice Games into one easy-to-manage book. Upon completion of the **All-In-One Piano Lessons Books C** and **D**, students will be ready to continue into Level 3 of the **Hal Leonard Student Piano Library.**

When music excites our interest and imagination, we eagerly put our hearts into learning it. The music in the **Hal Leonard Student Piano Library** encourages practice, progress, confidence, and best of all – success! Over 1,000 students and teachers in a nationwide test market responded with enthusiasm to the:

- variety of styles and moods
- natural rhythmic flow, singable melodies and lyrics
- "best ever" teacher accompaniments
- improvisations integrated throughout the **Lesson Books**
- orchestrated accompaniments included in audio and MIDI formats.

When new concepts have an immediate application to the music, the effort it takes to learn these skills seems worth it. Test market teachers and students were especially excited about the:

- "realistic" pacing that challenges without overwhelming
- clear and concise presentation of concepts that allows room for a teacher's individual approach
- uncluttered page layout that keeps the focus on the music.

The **Hal Leonard Student Piano Library** is the result of the efforts of many individuals. We extend our gratitude to all the teachers, students and colleagues who shared their energy and creative input. May this method guide your learning as you bring this music to life.

Best wishes,

Barbara Kreader   Fred Kern   Phillip Keveren   Mona Rejino

To access audio visit:
www.halleonard.com/mylibrary

Enter Code
2163-2543-7063-4866

ISBN 978-1-61780-690-2

HAL•LEONARD®
CORPORATION
7777 W. BLUEMOUND RD. P.O. BOX 13819 MILWAUKEE, WI 53213

CONTENTS

		Page No.	Audio Tracks

*✔

THE GRAND STAFF

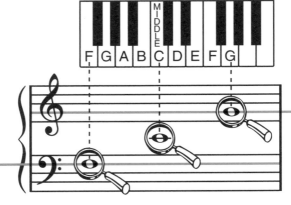

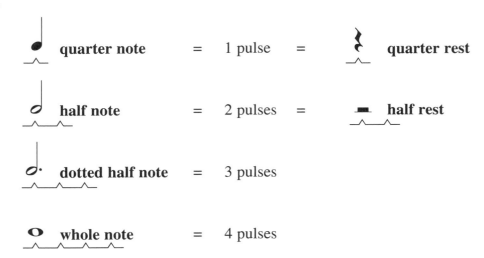

The **G note** is your reading guide for the **Treble or G Clef** (𝄞)

The **F note** is your reading guide for the **Bass or F Clef** (𝄢)

Middle C is your reading guide for the notes between the Treble and Bass Clefs.

NOTE VALUES

quarter note = 1 pulse = ❧ quarter rest

half note = 2 pulses = half rest

dotted half note = 3 pulses

whole note = 4 pulses

DYNAMIC SIGNS tell how loudly or softly to play and help create the mood of the music.

p (piano) = soft

mp (mezzo piano) = medium soft

mf (mezzo forte) = medium loud

f (forte) = loud

MUSICAL TERMS

time signatures $\frac{4}{4}$ $\frac{3}{4}$

repeat sign 𝄇

D.C. (Da Capo) al Fine means to return to the beginning (capo) and play until you see the sign for the end (fine).

steps

skips

tied notes

TEMPO MARKS tell the mood of the piece and the speed of the pulse.

Adagio
slowly

Andante
walking speed

Allegro
quickly

Musical Fitness Review

Use the following checklist to demonstrate the skills you learned in **All-In-One Books A** and **B**.

☐ **Sitting at the Piano**

Ask yourself:

- Am I sitting tall but staying relaxed?
- Are my wrists and elbows level with the keys of the piano?

☐ **Hand Position**

1. Let your arms and hands hang naturally at your sides. Notice the curve of your fingers.

2. Keep this position as you place your fingers on the keys.

When you are playing the piano, keep your fingers in this curved position.

3. When playing with your thumb, let it rest naturally on its outside tip.

☐ **Beautiful Tone**
Place the weight of your whole arm behind each finger as you play.
Let your arm follow your fingers and listen for an even sound on each note.

☐ **Attention to Silence**
Release your arm weight during each rest, keeping your fingers on the keys.

☐ **Playing *Forte***
Press the key to the bottom of the key bed with full arm weight.

☐ **Playing *Piano***
Press the key to the bottom of the key bed with less arm weight.

☐ **Detached Tones**
Release the key as soon as you play it, letting your wrist bounce lightly.
Notice how your finger naturally rebounds and comes to rest on the key.

☐ **Connected Tones**
Pass the sound smoothly from finger to finger or hand to hand.

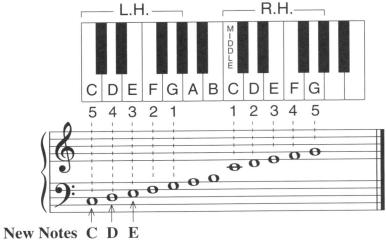

New Notes C D E

WHOLE REST

▬

means to rest for
an entire measure.

Remember,

Whenever you see
this magnifying glass,
fill in the name of the
note.

Reflection

Barbara Kreader

Moderately

mp Am I the re - flec - tion in the mir - ror on the wall?

Or is the re - flec - tion in the mir - ror who I am?

Accompaniment (Student plays one octave higher than written.) 🔊 1/2

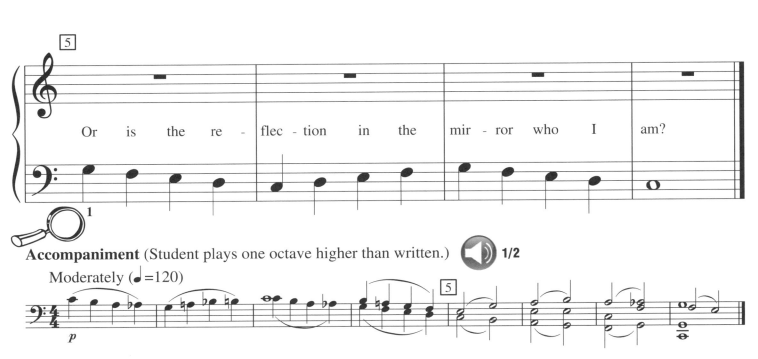

Moderately (♩=120)

p

6

The Grand Staff – A Musical Map

Help Inspector Hound complete his map.

1. Write the names of the blank keys on the keyboard.
2. Trace the missing notes on the staff.
3. Color the following keys on the keyboard and notes on the staff:

   Red for C   Blue for D   Green for E

Write the note names in the blanks below.
Your teacher will play one measure from each blue box. Circle the example you hear.

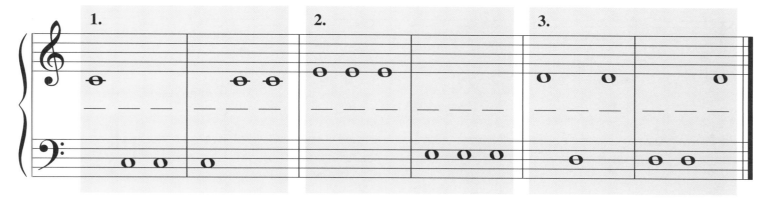

Teacher's Examples on pg. 79

My Own Song
On C D E F G

Place both hands on C D E F G. Listen and feel the pulse as your teacher plays the accompaniment below.

With your right hand, play C D E F G and then play G F E D C. Experiment by mixing the letters any way you want and make up your own song!

With your left hand, play C D E F G and then play G F E D C. Again, mix the letters any way you want and make up another song!

Have fun!

Accompaniment 3
Moderately (♩=120)

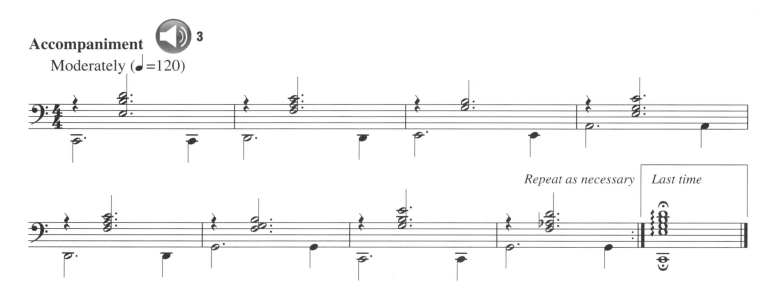

Repeat as necessary | *Last time*

Ode To Joy

Ludwig van Beethoven
(1770–1827)
Adapted by Fred Kern

Accompaniment (Student plays one octave higher than written.)  **4/5**

With majesty (♩=105)

Drawing Notes on the Staff

Practice drawing stems.

Notes on the third line and higher have stems on the left going down.

Notes on the second space and lower have stems on the right going up.

Add a stem to each note.

Add a stem to each note.

Spike is conducting *Ode To Joy*. Help him write the cello part. It is written in the bass clef and uses the same notes as the melody in the violin part. Draw the missing notes in the blue boxes.

violin

cello

Play the two parts hands separately, then hands together.

Rope Bridge

Smoothly

Accompaniment (Student plays one octave higher than written.) **6/7**

Smoothly (♩=120)

Rests

When Pig and Goat tried to play *Old MacDonald Had A Farm*,
they had trouble because the rests were missing!

Trace and fill in each rest and draw three more.

Quarter Rest **Half Rest** **Whole Rest**

Help Pig and Goat complete each measure by drawing the correct rest in each blue box.

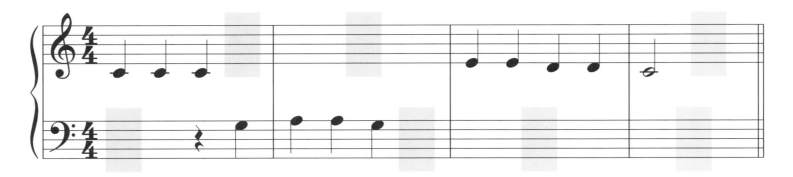

Listen & Respond

🔊 8/9

Carmen's Tune
(Activity Page)

As you listen to *Carmen's Tune*, tap the following rhythm:

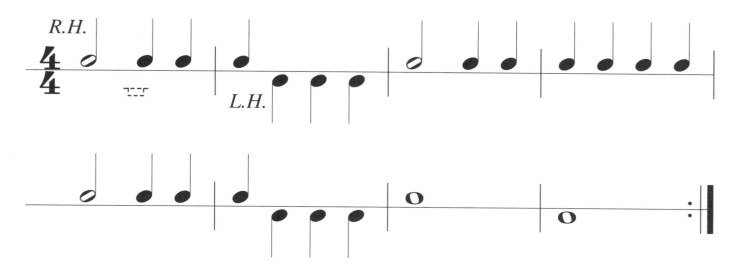

Read & Discover

The Beat Goes On!

When the melody passes from one hand to the other, the beat goes on. While one hand plays, the other hand rests. Using pg. 14 as a guide, add the missing rests to the rhythm of the melody above.

Carmen's Tune

Georges Bizet
(1838–1875)
Adapted by Fred Kern

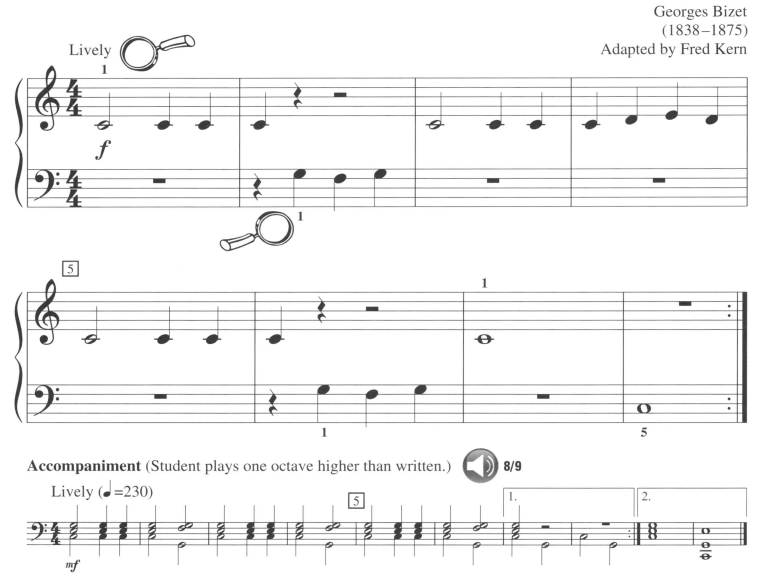

Accompaniment (Student plays one octave higher than written.) 8/9

Playing on C D E F G

Party Cat is trying to trick you by playing one wrong note in each song below.
Play each song. As your teacher plays Party Cat's version of each one,
circle the one note he plays wrong.

1.

2.

3.

4.

5.

Teacher's Examples on pg. 79

Magnet March

Stepping steady

Phillip Keveren

Accompaniment (Student plays one octave higher than written.) 🔊 **10/11**

Stepping steady (♩ = 120)

mf detached

Remember,

3/4 TIME SIGNATURE

3/4 = three beats fill every measure
= quarter note gets one beat

Andantino

LEGATO

When notes sound smooth and connected, they are **Legato**.

A curved line over or under several notes (slur) means **Legato**.

To play **Legato**, pass the sound smoothly from one finger to the next.

*Andantino  12/13

Louis Köhler
(1820–1886)
Adapted by Fred Kern

* *Andantino means a slightly faster tempo than Andante.*

17

Song Of The Orca

Singing, with mystery

Phillip Keveren

Come   and   play   with   me,   Jes - sie,   Jes - sie.

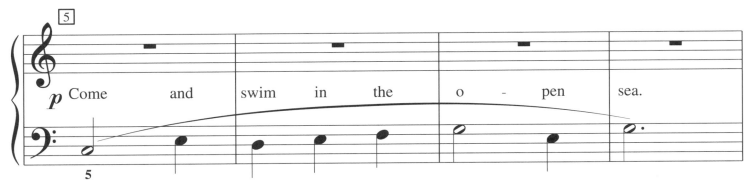

Come   and   swim   in   the   o - pen   sea.

Accompaniment (Student plays two octaves higher than written.)   14/15

Singing, with mystery (♩=125)

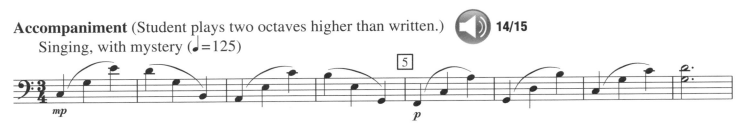

Ride with me to our se - cret is - land.

Jes - sie, Jes - sie, come and play in the sea.

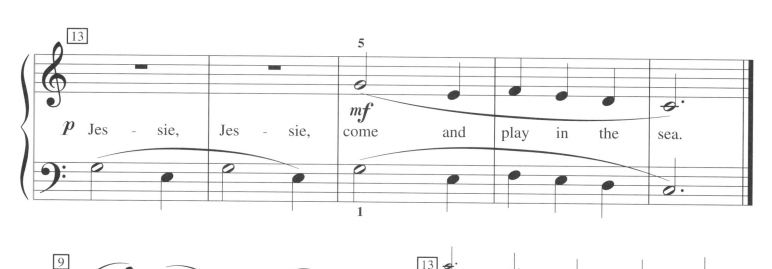

Rhythm Detective

Find the missing measures!

Each rhythm in Column A is missing its second measure. You will find it in Column B.

Your teacher will clap each two-measure pattern. Connect the first measure in Column A to the correct second measure in Column B.

A   **B**

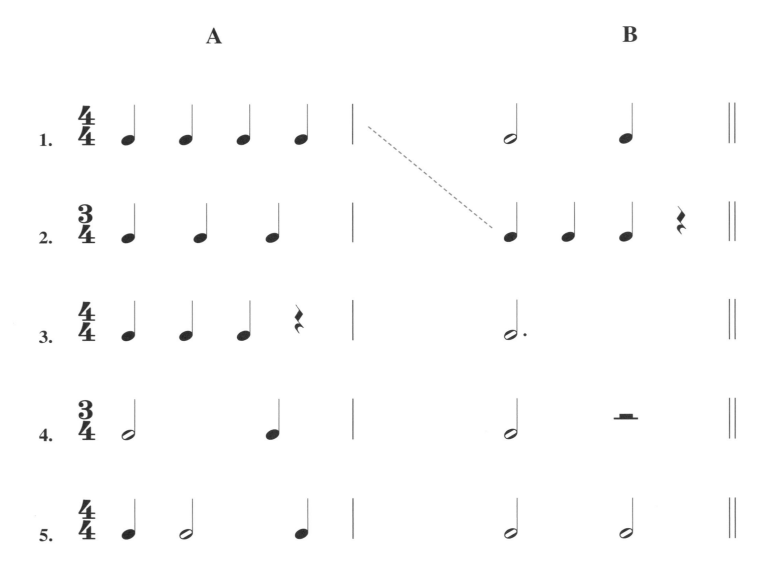

Teacher's Examples on pg. 79

Remember,

TIES

A **Tie** is a curved line that connects two notes of the same pitch. Hold one sound for the combined value of both notes.

Big Ben

Steady (♩=120) 🔊 **16/17**

Traditional

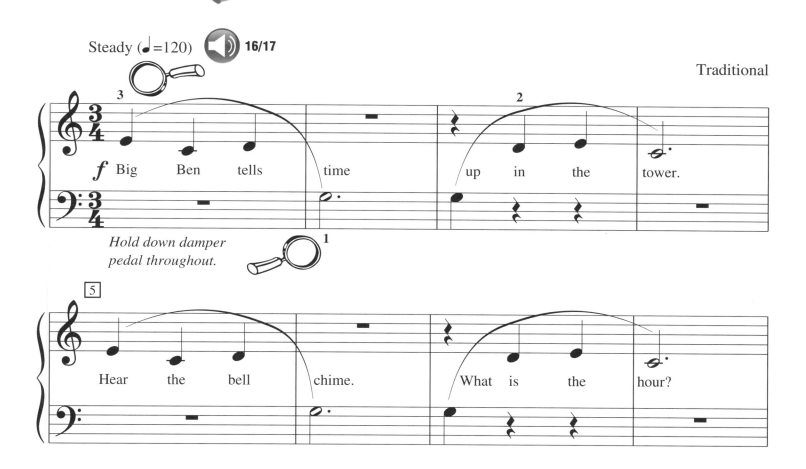

Hold down damper pedal throughout.

f Big Ben tells time up in the tower.

Hear the bell chime. What is the hour?

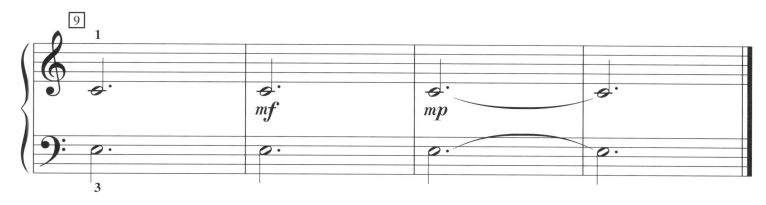

Note Name Review

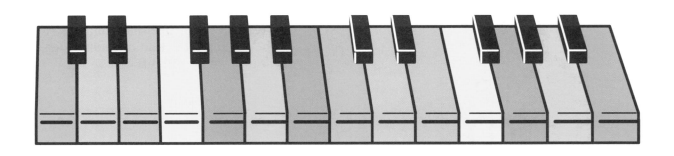

Complete this picture using the colors in the keyboard guide.

 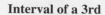

With your left hand play:

Melodic 2nds   Harmonic 2nds   Melodic 3rds   Harmonic 3rds

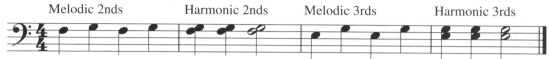

Please, No Bees!

Cranky (♩=155)   18/19

Barbara Kreader

mf Please, no bees!   Please, no bees   on my nose or

neck or knees!   Bring no sting!   Bring no sting!

Find a rose,   not my nose!   Ouch! *f*

*Lowest C
on the piano.*

23

Harmonic or Melodic?

Each of Party Cat's balloons has either a melodic or harmonic interval.
Circle the correct answer.

Clapping Song

Bouncy (♩=140) 🔊 **20/21**

Guatemalan

f Feel the beat with me in this clap-ping song.

Eas-y as can be, keep it loud and strong.

The Macaroni Cha-Cha

With gusto

Phillip Keveren

We love chees-y mac-a-ro-ni, We real-ly

mf

LOVE that chees-y mac-a-ro-ni. (Cha-cha-cha.) Well,

Accompaniment (Student plays one octave higher than written.) 22/23

With gusto (♩ = 190)

mp

Harmonic 2nds and 3rds

In each of Spike's balloons, draw a whole note that is a
harmonic 2nd or 3rd above each given note.

Bee Cha-Cha

Bouncy

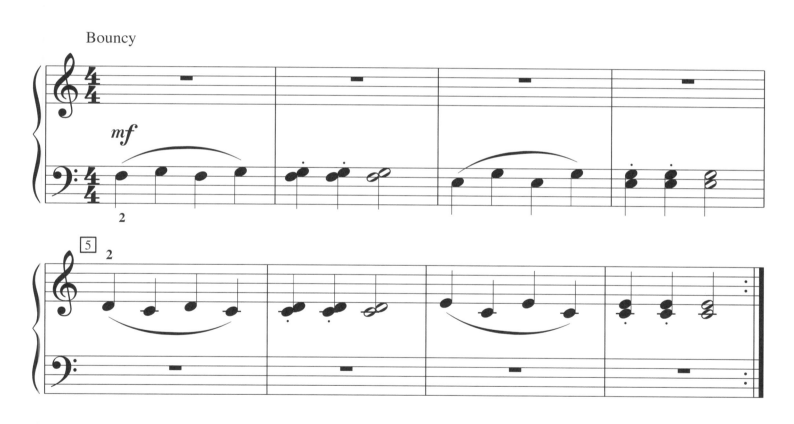

Accompaniment (Student plays two octaves higher than written.) 24/25

Bouncy (♩=130)

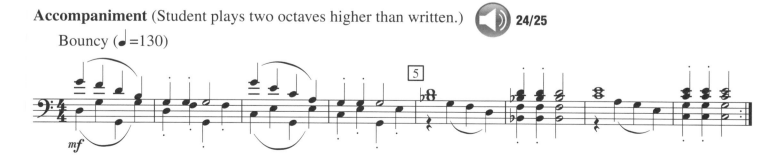

Drawing Legato and Staccato Marks

Bear has composed some music.
Help him add the legato marks (slurs)
or staccato marks to each example.

1. Add slurs to each phrase, then play this song.
2. Circle the best song title.

Skating

Popping Corn

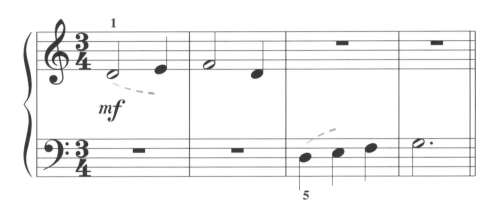

1. Add a staccato mark to each note, then play this song.
2. Circle the best song title.

Jumping Jacks

Sliding

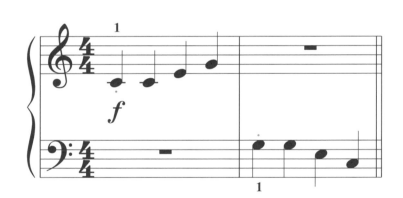

Match the mood of these titles by adding either slurs or staccato marks to the music.

Sneaking on Tiptoe   **Smooth as Silk**

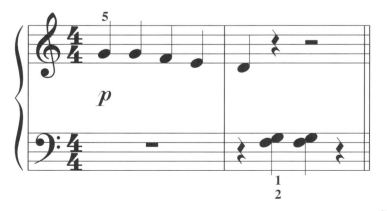

30

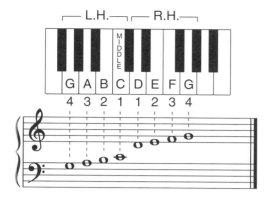

INTERVAL of a 4th

On the piano, a 4th
- skips two keys
- skips two fingers
- skips two letters

On the staff, a 4th
- skips two notes from either a line to a space or a space to a line.

Hoedown

Janet Medley

Toe tappin'

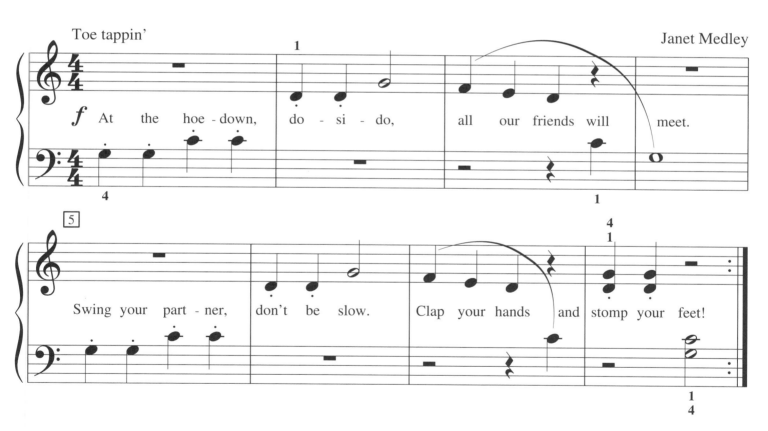

f At the hoe - down, do - si - do, all our friends will meet.

Swing your part - ner, don't be slow. Clap your hands and stomp your feet!

Accompaniment (Student plays one octave higher than written.) 🔊 **26/27**

Toe tappin' (♩=150)

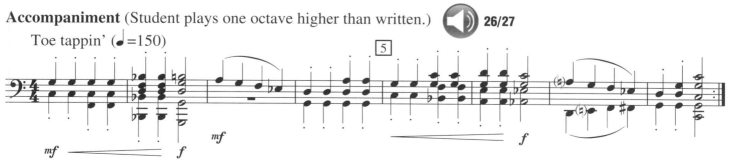

mf   *f*   *mf*   *f*

4ths

Match each 4th on the staff to the same 4th on the keyboard
by drawing a line from Column A to Column B.

A

B

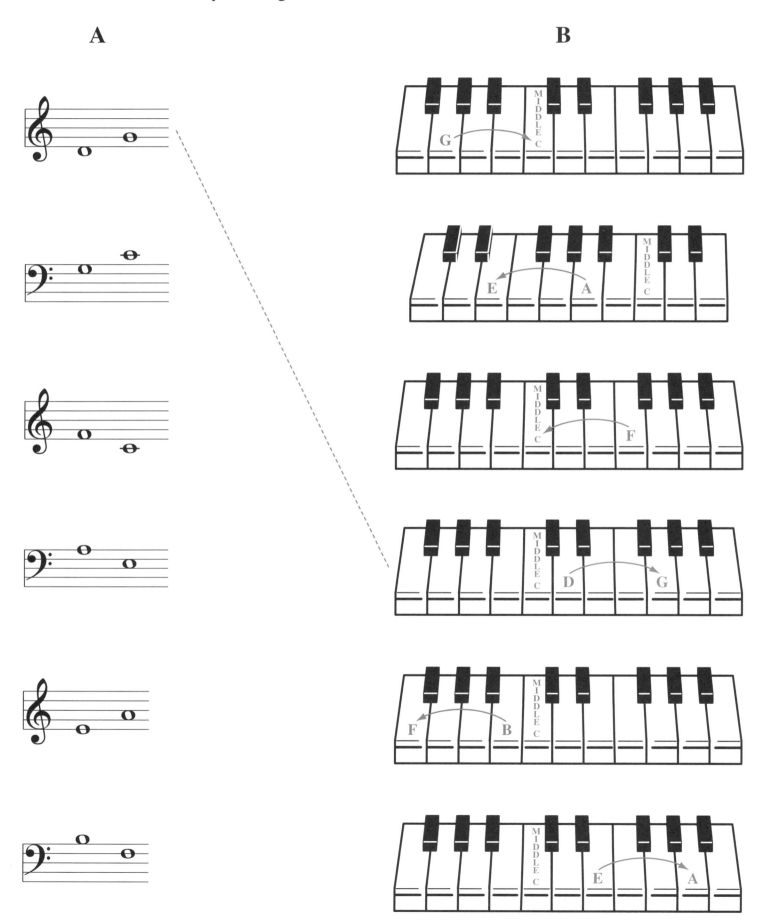

Sunlight Through The Trees

Flowing (♩=120) 28/29

Phillip Keveren

Play one octave higher than written and hold down damper pedal throughout.

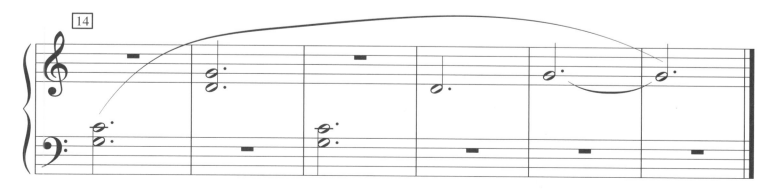

Sunlight Through The Trees
(Activity Page)

Imagine & Create

1. **Put the pieces back together!**

   Cut out the cards on the next page and arrange them in the correct order of the piece, *Sunlight Through The Trees.*

2. **Create a new piece!**

   Begin with the card showing the clef signs and the time signature.

   Arrange the groups of notes in any order you wish.

   Place the card with the double bar at the end of the piece.

3. **Give your composition a title!**

   Save your new piece by taping it on a piece of cardboard.

Title:_____

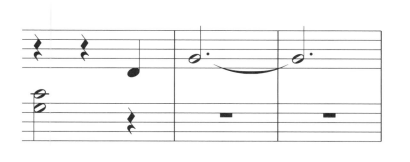

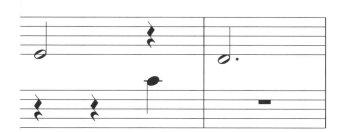

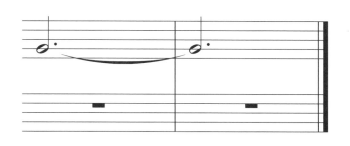

Intervalasaurus

Complete this picture by drawing a straight line from one note to the next.
Write the name of the intervals in the blue boxes.

The Stream

Gently rippling

Phillip Keveren

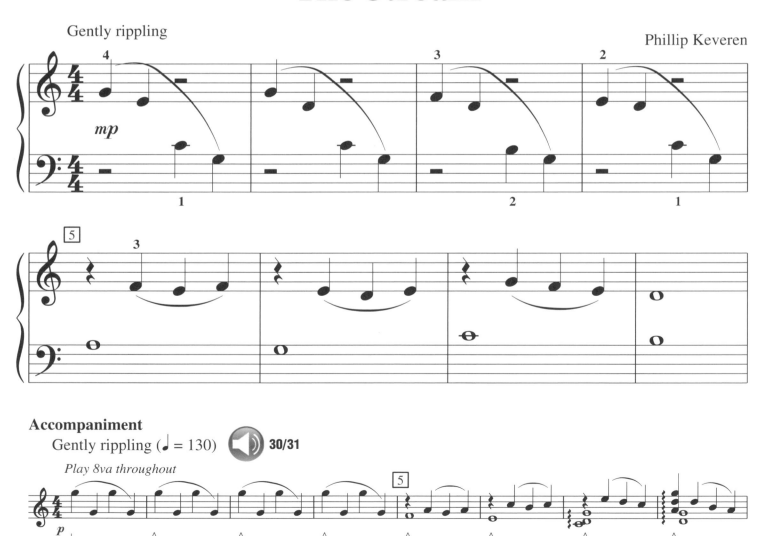

Accompaniment

Gently rippling (♩ = 130) 30/31

Play 8va throughout

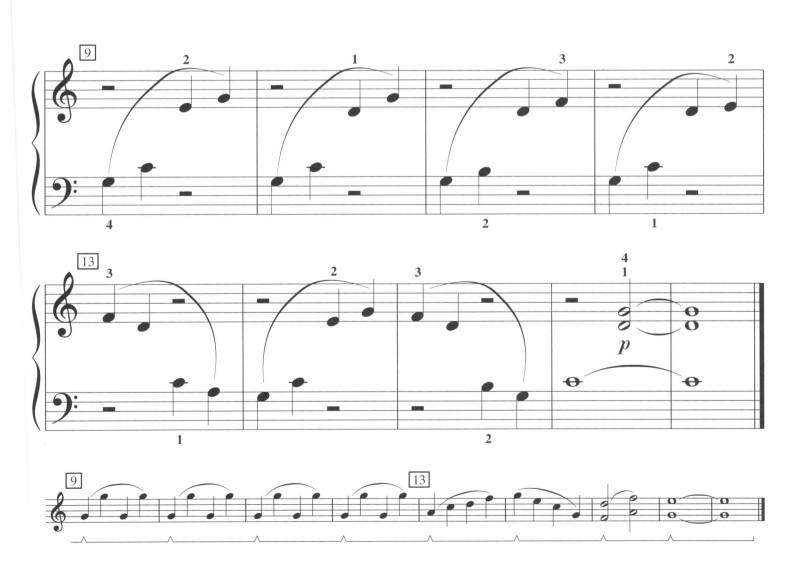

UPBEAT (Pick-up)

Notes that come before the first full measure are called **Upbeats**.

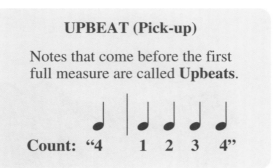

Count: "4   1   2   3   4"

Bingo

Bouncy

Traditional

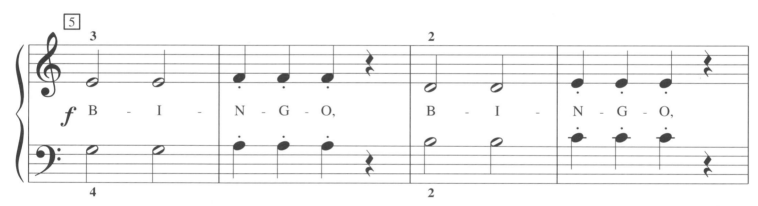

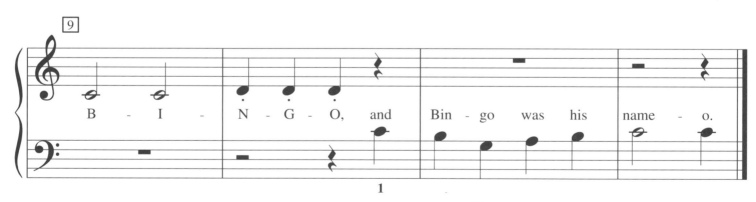

Accompaniment (Student plays one octave higher than written.) **32/33**

Bouncy (♩=140)

Upbeat Melodies

Party Cat needs to sharpen his rhythmic skills before his next jam session.

1. Write the correct time signature in each blue box.
2. Write the counts in the blanks.
3. Play each melody.

1.

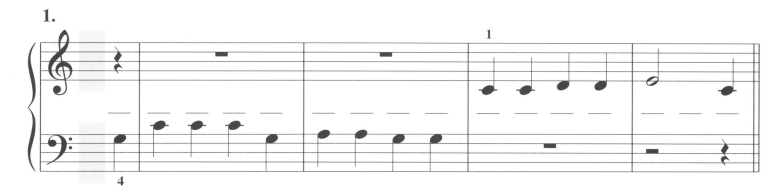

2.

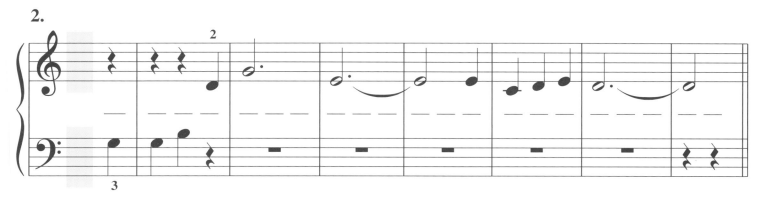

3.

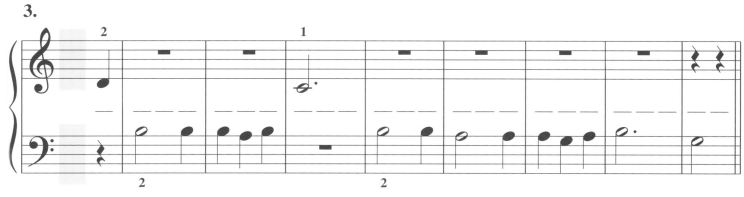

Measuring Upbeats

Duck is playing the drums for an upcoming dance at Spike's house.
Help him add the bar lines to his music. Every example has an upbeat.

1. Trace the barline that separates the upbeat from the
   first full measure. Then add bar lines to complete
   each example. Because of the upbeat, the last
   measure will be incomplete.
2. Clap and count each pattern.

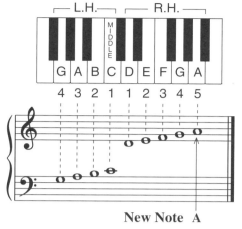

New Note A

Travelling Along
The Prairie

Italo Taranta

Accompaniment (Student plays one octave higher than written.) 🔊 **34/35**

Moving along (♩=145)

43

Imagine & Create

Orange Horizon
(Improv Activity)

Get ready to improvise!

Place your hands in the *Travelling Along The Prairie* position and get ready to improvise a new piece titled *Orange Horizon*.

1. Practice playing this repeated accompaniment (ostinato) with your L.H.

Repeat as necessary

2. After you can play the accompaniment easily, improvise a R.H. melody with the notes D E G A. Try playing your melody one octave higher.

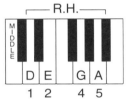

Orange Horizon

Quietly

Repeat as necessary

p

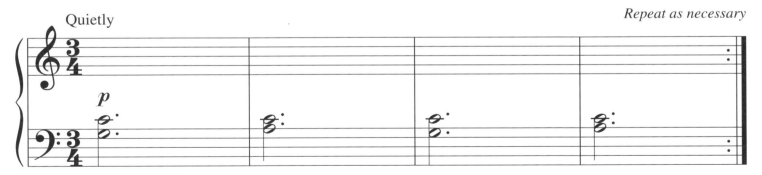

Hold damper pedal down throughout.

3. When you are ready to end your piece, rest your R.H. and let the L.H. accompaniment continue. Gradually fade away by playing softer and softer, slower and slower.

Leaps And Bounds

Moderato (♩ = 155)  36/37

Italo Taranta

Out To Sea

We're sail - ing out to sea, _____ just

Par - ty Cat and me. _____ But he for - got the

boat, _____ I'm glad that we can float! _____

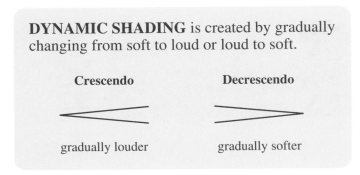

DYNAMIC SHADING is created by gradually changing from soft to loud or loud to soft.

Crescendo

gradually louder

Decrescendo

gradually softer

No One To Walk With

Slowly

Italo Taranta

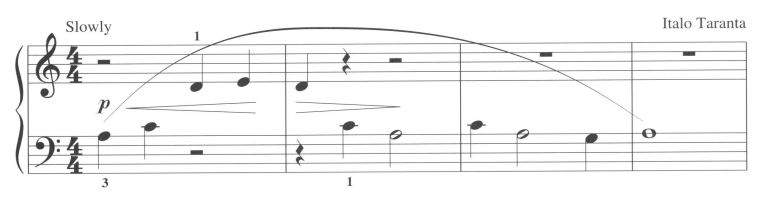

Accompaniment (Student plays one octave higher than written.) 🔊 **40/41**

Slowly (♩=100)

48

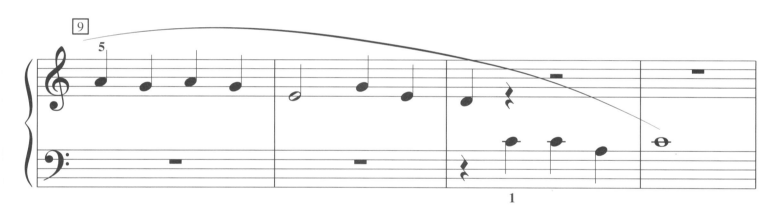

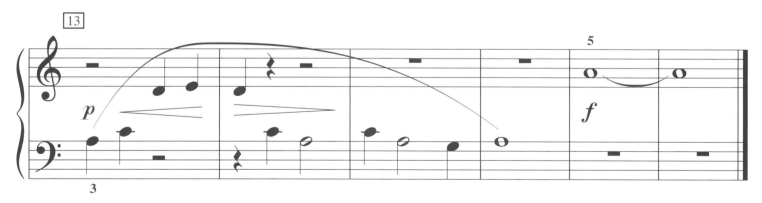

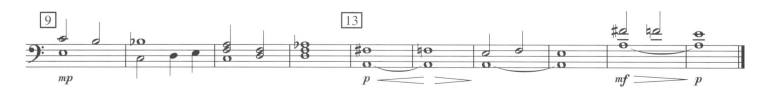

49

Expression Marks

Certain musical signs, such as 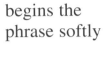 (*crescendo*) and 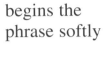 (*decrescendo*), tell us how to play the notes in a way that creates the mood of the music.

1. Sing *No One To Walk With* on "la" using one breath for each phrase.
   Be sure that your voice:

| begins the phrase softly | rises to a slightly louder level | and softly fades away at the end |

2. Imitate this effect on the piano by passing the sound from one finger to the next, creating a slight *crescendo* and *decrescendo* within each phrase.

Extra for Experts!

Study and compare the four phrases and circle the correct answers:

1. Which phrases are exactly alike?   1   2   3   4

2. Which phrase begins with an upbeat?   1   2   3   4

3. Which phrases include the melodic interval
   of a fourth?   1   2   3   4

Mirage

Accompaniment (Student plays one octave higher than written.) 🔊 **42/43**

Painted Rocking Horse

Phillip Keveren

Dreamlike

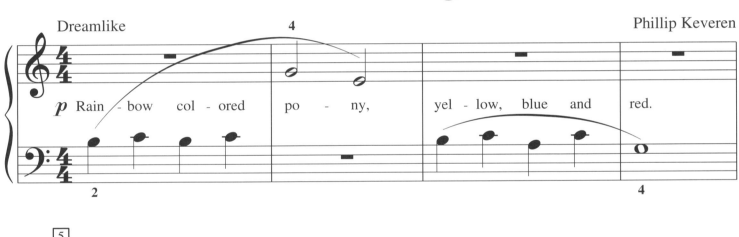

p Rain - bow col - ored po - ny, yel - low, blue and red.

Al - ways here be - side me, stand - ing by my bed.

Accompaniment (Student plays two octaves higher than written.) 44/45

Dreamlike (♩=95)

With pedal

When the sky is cloud - y, you and I can play,

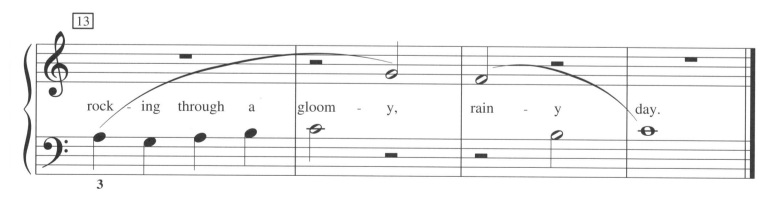

rock - ing through a gloom - y, rain - y day.

Dynamic Detective

Add your own dynamic marks to the music below.

1. Play each piece below.

2. Choose either *p*, *f* or *ff* and draw the symbol in the ▢ boxes in measures 1 and 4.

3. Choose either ⊂ or ⊃ and draw the symbol in the ▢ box in measure 3.

Painted Rocking Horse

Hoedown

54

Painted Rocking Horse
(Activity Page)

Many measures of the music look alike, but if you are a good detective, you will find the differences between them.

1. Play each of these examples:

Ex. 1

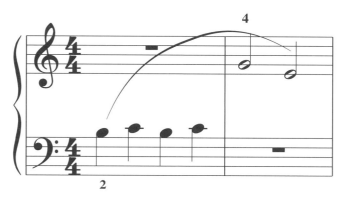

Ex. 2

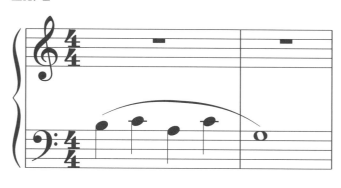

Ex. 3

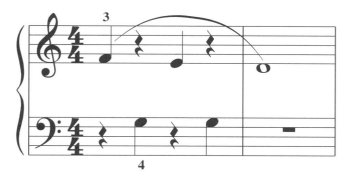

Ex. 4

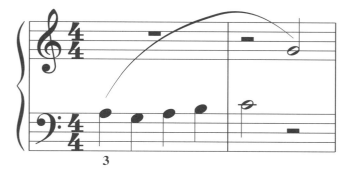

2. Circle the correct answers:

Which example begins in the R.H.?	1	2	3	4
Which example has no B in it?	1	2	3	4
Which example uses only the L.H.?	1	2	3	4
Which examples end on G?	1	2	3	4

Tick Tock The Jazz Clock

With a steady beat like the tick of a clock

Bill Boyd

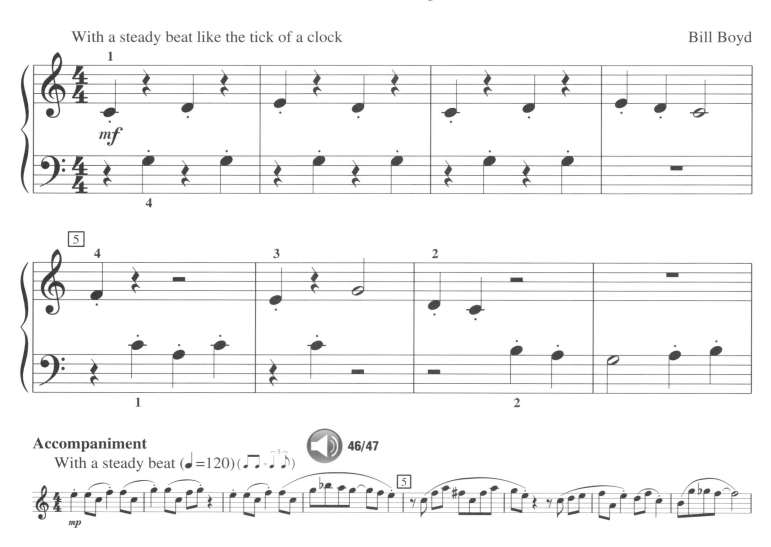

Accompaniment

With a steady beat (♩=120)

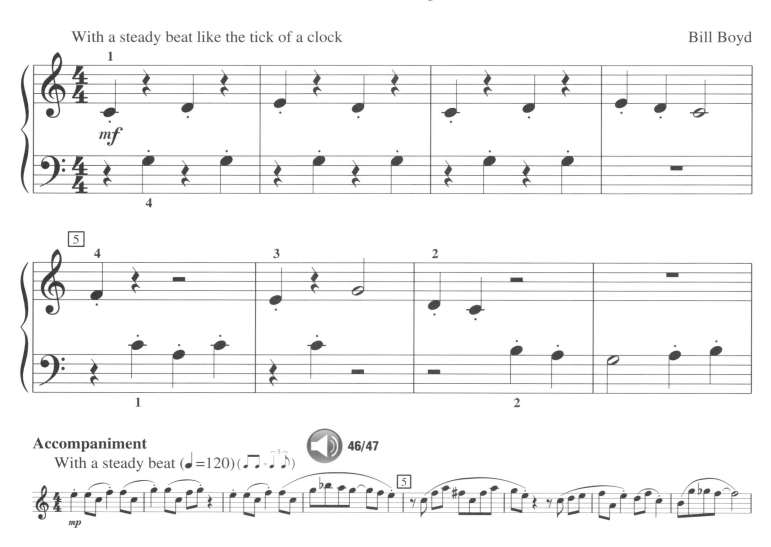

46/47

W Rong Rhythms

Sometimes Party Cat forgets to wind the Jazz Clock and its rhythmic ticking gets mixed up.

Each measure below should have four counts. Put an "X" through any of the measures that have the wrong number of counts.

1.

2.

3.

4.

5.

6.

Prancing

Lightly

mf

Accompaniment (Student plays two octaves higher than written.) 48/49

Lightly (♩=145)

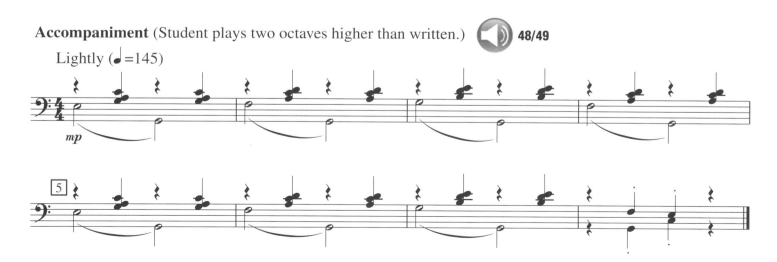

mp

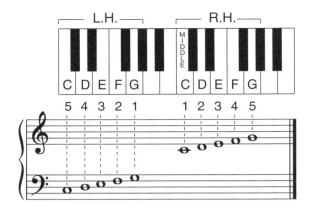

INTERVAL of a 5th

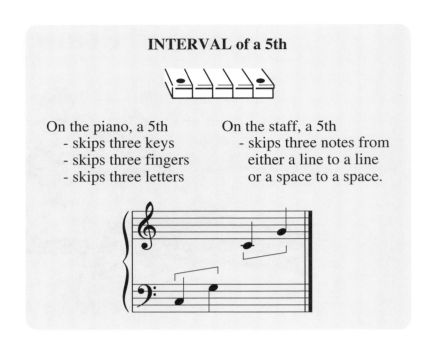

On the piano, a 5th
- skips three keys
- skips three fingers
- skips three letters

On the staff, a 5th
- skips three notes from either a line to a line or a space to a space.

Watercolors

Delicately (♩=105)   Phillip Keveren

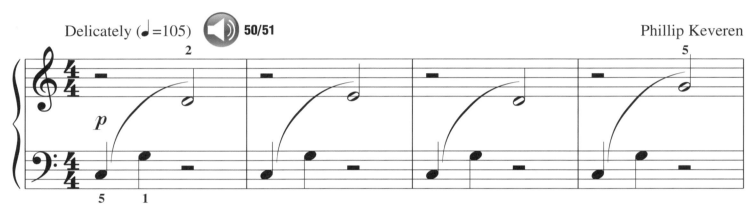

Play one octave higher than written and hold down damper pedal throughout.

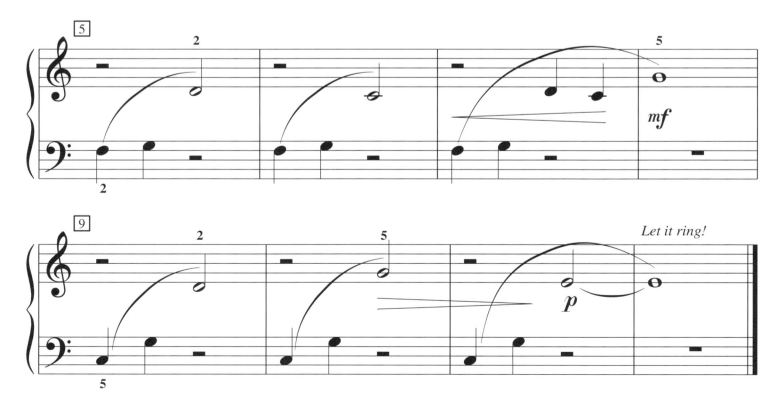

 50/51

Watercolors
(Technique Tune)

Technique Tunes

As you listen to *Watercolors*, play the following **Technique Tune** three times:

1) as written
2) one octave higher
3) two octaves higher

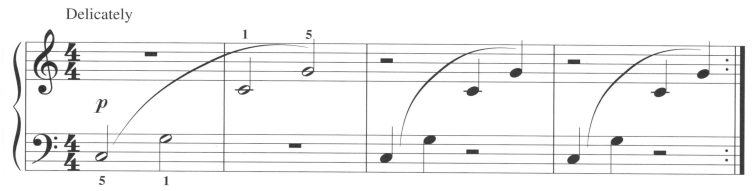

Delicately

p

Hold down damper pedal throughout.

Note: As a duet, the teacher plays "Watercolors" two octaves higher, and the student plays the Technique Tune three times as written.

Imagine & Create

🔊 50/51

Watercolors
(Improv Activity)

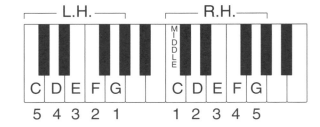

All that's missing is you!

Place your hands in the *Watercolors* hand position. As you listen to *Watercolors*, make up your own melody using the notes C D E F G in the empty measures. Play in the rhythm shown.

Beeline to the Intervals

1. Draw a line from each bee to a flower that matches it.
2. Color the flowers using this guide:

| 2nds Orange | 3rds Blue | 4ths Yellow | 5ths Red |

63

Listen & Respond

 52/53

Circle Dance
(Technique Tune)

> **TWO-NOTE SLURS**
>
> A **Two-Note Slur** is a curved line over or under two notes of different pitch. It means to play smoothly, connecting the notes by passing the sound from the first finger to the second (legato).

Technique Tunes

As you listen to *Circle Dance*, play the following **Technique Tune**. Connect the two-note slurs by using one continuous arm movement to pass the sound from one finger to the next. During each rest, relax your energy, keeping your fingers ready to play the next notes.

Note: As a duet, the teacher plays "Circle Dance" two octaves higher.

Circle Dance

Lively (♩=165) 52/53

Phillip Keveren

'Round in a cir - cle we spin to the mel - o - dy,

diz - zy and diz - zi - er, 'til we fall down!

mf

mp

Fine

D.C. al Fine

Outside-In

Moving along

Accompaniment (Student plays one octave higher than written.) 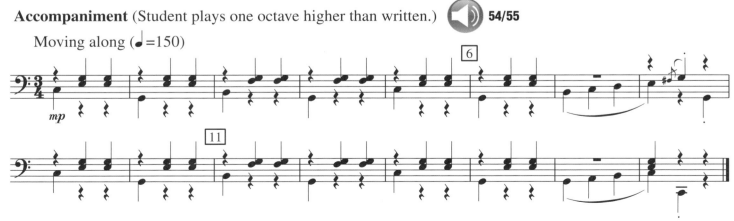 🔊 **54/55**

Moving along (♩=150)

Inside-Out

Accompaniment (Student plays one octave higher than written.) 🔊 **56/57**

67

Ties or Slurs?

Study each example.
Are the notes connected by a tie or a slur?
Circle the correct answer.

A **tie** is a curved line that connects notes of the **same** pitch.

A **slur** is a curved line that connects notes of **different** pitch.

tie   slur

tie   slur

tie   slur

tie   slur

tie   slur

tie   slur

tie   slur

tie   slur

tie   slur

Interval Bounce

Measure the distance of each basketball bounce.

1. Put a "1" in each blue ball and continue counting every space and line to the next brown basketball. Write the name of each interval in the box below each basketball.

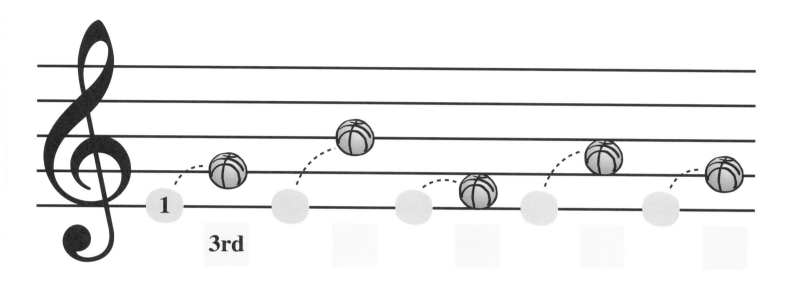

1

3rd

2. Put a "1" in each blue ball. Draw a basketball on the line or space that matches the name of the interval.

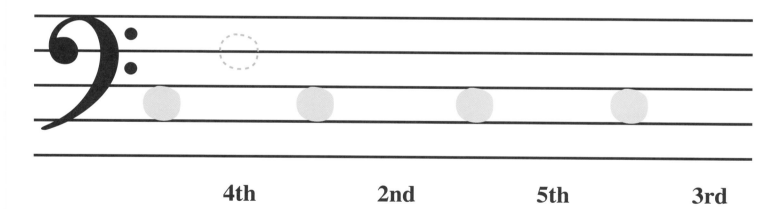

4th   **2nd**   **5th**   **3rd**

Basketball Bounce

Tempo de dribble (With energy!) (♩=190) 58/59

Phillip Keveren

Basketball Bounce

(Activity Page)

 58/59

1. As you listen to *Basketball Bounce*, imitate the sound of a basketball bouncing back and forth between hands by tapping this rhythm:

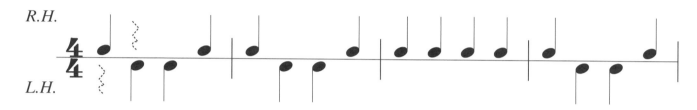

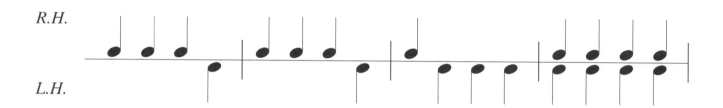

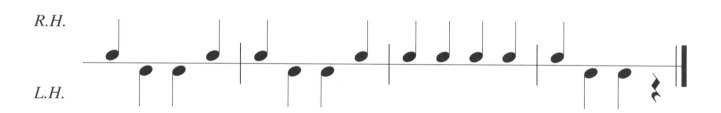

Pass the Beat!

2. While one hand plays the beat, the other hand rests. Using your lesson book as a guide, write in the missing rests.

Dance Of The Court Jester

Bill Boyd

With humor

Accompaniment 60/61

With humor ($\quad$ = 160)

Allegro

Anton Diabelli
(1781–1858)
Adapted by Fred Kern

It's a Tie!

Some rhythms sound the same but <u>look</u> different.
Match the measures that sound alike by drawing a line
from Column A to Column B.

A   B

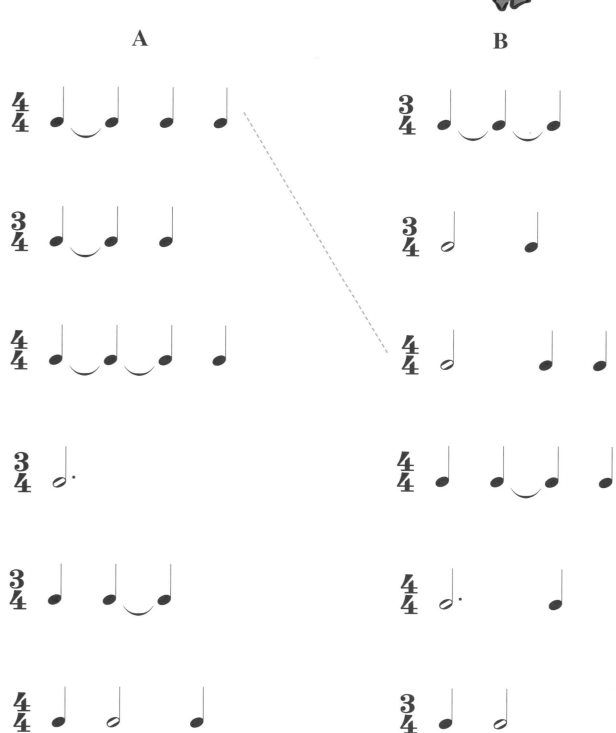

Listen & Respond

🔊 **64/65**

Great News!
(Technique Tune)

As you listen to *Great News!*, play this **Technique Tune** two octaves higher than written.

With excitement!   *Play throughout the piece.*

Read & Discover

1. Measure 13 uses the same notes as measure 14.
   Practice these measures until you can play them easily.

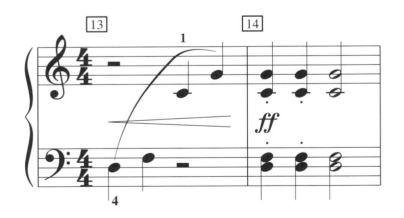

2. Circle the correct answers.

The intervals in measure 13 are:	**melodic**		**harmonic**	
The intervals in measure 14 are:	**melodic**		**harmonic**	
The L.H. plays an interval of a:	**2nd**	**3rd**	**4th**	**5th**
The R.H. plays an interval of a:	**2nd**	**3rd**	**4th**	**5th**

Great News!

With excitement! (♩=170) 64/65

Bruce Berr

Brass Fanfare

Triumphantly (♩=110) 66/67

Phillip Keveren

Teacher's Examples

Page 7 (Play)

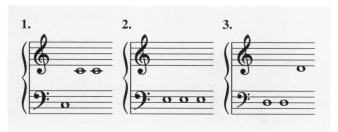

Page 15 (Play)   * = Party Cat's wrong note.

Page 20 (Clap)

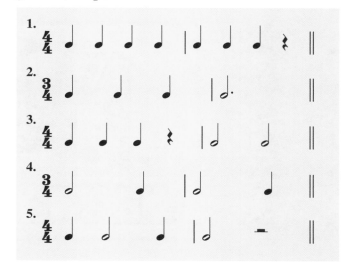

HAS SUCCESSFULLY COMPLETED

HAL LEONARD ALL-IN-ONE

PIANO LESSONS, BOOK C

AND

IS HEREBY PROMOTED TO

ALL-IN-ONE BOOK D

TEACHER   DATE

HAL•LEONARD®